contents

Learning Agility in Action

It was early 2014, and the Ebola virus was beginning its deadly spread through portions of Western Africa. As the outbreak crept ever closer to Liberia's crowded capital, Monrovia, Dr. Jerry Brown, medical director of the ELWA hospital, was concerned. What might be the consequences of the outbreak in a city of over four million people, with only a handful of ambulances and no established isolation wards?

Dr. Brown realized that something needed to be done and quickly translated his concerns into action. Without any direct training in the treatment of the virus and no infectious disease experts in the country to reach out to, Dr. Brown and his team went about preparing themselves—not yet knowing the scope of the problem that would eventually come their way.

When the virus reached Monrovia, Dr. Brown and his team immediately found themselves fighting multiple battles. Before the first ambulance arrived, staff were refusing to administer treatment and even resigning. Dr. Brown had to persuade staff and lead by example to help overcome others' fears and uncertainties. That was just the beginning. Government officials, aid agencies, suppliers, and others all had to be called upon and persuaded to lend their efforts to stemming the crisis.

Furthermore, the virus itself was extremely difficult to contain and treat. The initial small number of cases quickly multiplied into a full-blown outbreak. Instincts and resourcefulness were as much in play as medical knowledge and training. Dr. Brown and his team had to improvise protocols and treatments, and when these approaches didn't work, they reassessed the situation and tried a new approach.

As weeks passed, ELWA's patients began showing signs of recovery, and surviving patients were eventually discharged. To win the confidence of the media and the public, Dr. Brown took the bold move of shaking hands with survivors to symbolize that the virus could indeed be overcome. The outbreak was not without its devastating toll, but ELWA eventually discharged 234 patients and, while some medical staff did become ill, they were among the survivors.

Dr. Brown and several others who heroically fought the Ebola outbreak were recognized for their efforts by being named as Time magazine's Person of the Year for 2014. In a video interview with the magazine, Dr. Brown reflected: "There's a lot of things I've really learned from this outbreak. One of which is being able to look around yourself and see what you can use that's available. To find a remedy to the situation [rather] than just sitting and waiting for a remedy from outside. What's in your power. How you can make use of what's available."

The story of Dr. Brown and the staff at ELWA is an inspiring account of courage, resilience, and determination to triumph in the face of enormous challenges. It is also a vivid example of the mindset and behaviors that characterize learning agility.

"How do they do that?"

You know the type. Give them a fresh challenge and somehow, like Dr. Brown and his team, they find a pathway to success. Nothing in particular about their skills or expertise would make them a natural fit to succeed, yet they seem to thrive no matter the circumstances. Stumbles? Setbacks? Not an issue. In fact, they bounce back from failure time after time and often come back better than ever.

It's a rare and valuable talent. These individuals make a name for themselves as the go-to leaders in situations where the stakes are high, the problems lack clarity, and the solutions aren't easy to identify, much less execute: starting up an overseas operation, implementing a complex new technology, turning around an underperforming product line, leading a postmerger integration team.

Success in these types of situations often leads to opportunities to once again lead the organization into the unknown, take on daunting risks, and achieve the success that has eluded others. As a result, the careers of these individuals resemble less a steady climb up the ladder than a series of adventures that lead both them and the organization to new and exciting places.

But what is it that these people do to make them such unique and special talents? Some characteristics come to mind—curious, insightful, resourceful, adaptable, savvy, resilient—but no single one seems to capture what sets them apart. That's because it's not a single trait, but rather an integrated set of behaviors, that underlies their success.

3

Through decades of research, CCL has gained insight into the exact nature of these behaviors, collectively called learning agility. We also understand how these behaviors can be developed. What's more, while many people don't possess high levels of learning agility, it can be learned and anyone can become more proficient.

This book will decode the mystery behind learning-agile individuals' abilities and put you on the path to developing these abilities for yourself. At the heart of learning agility is something that we all have but we might not always see or leverage the value in—our experience. Through the information, exercises, and tools captured here, you'll learn a new way to think about, approach, and apply your experiences.

We'll use some of the experiences you've already had as a learning tool to guide you through the core elements of developing your learning agility. So, before you go any further, take a moment to reflect and respond to the questions that follow.

First, think about a specific experience where you were at your best and the outcomes were positive. Briefly describe the situation and the end result.

MY POSITIVE EXPERIENCE

How would you describe the situation?

....

....

....

What was the end result?

....

....

....

Second, think about another experience where, by contrast, you were far from your best and the outcomes were negative. Briefly describe the situation and the end result below.

MY NEGATIVE EXPERIENCE

How would you describe the situation?

....

....

....

What was the end result?

....

....

....

We'll revisit these experiences and explore them more deeply at various points throughout the book. But next, let's learn more about why experience is so valuable and the role it plays in developing your learning agility.

The Essential (But Incomplete) Role of Experience

Score one for conventional wisdom: CCL research shows that experience is indeed the best teacher. Specifically, we derive significantly more value in what we learn from our own experiences than from what we learn through others (bosses, colleagues, coaches, etc.) or formal learning (courses, training, etc.). Academic researchers and organizational practitioners now recognize that a deliberate focus on learning from experience is one of the most valuable approaches to developing the leadership skills that drive long-term career success.

Three aspects of our experience make this learning even more valuable. The first is quantity. The sheer number of distinct learning experiences we've accumulated provides us with the "raw material" for learning. The more experiences, the better for potential learning. The second is quality, or richness, of experience. Not all learning experiences are equal. Experiences with characteristics such as novelty, complexity, and high stakes offer greater opportunity for learning than those that are familiar, straightforward, and low risk. Third, diversity of experience matters. The more we encounter new types of people and situations that require different skills for success, the more we can potentially learn.

We'll explore these aspects in more detail later. For now, it's important to understand that while quantity, quality, and diversity of experience are very important, experience alone is not enough. There's one more critical variable to take into account—some individuals excel relative to others in their ability to learn from their experience.

Let's use an example to illustrate. Jamie and Kim are members of a team that just spent several months designing and launching a new product that they hope will open up new markets for their company. As they wound down the project and prepared themselves for new assignments, they each reflected on the insights they had gained from the experience. Here are Jamie's takeaways (the big "Aha's" are in bold, and more subtle lessons are in normal type):

THINGS I LEARNED ABOUT DOING MY JOB:

- **Prototype early and often.**
- **Get a clear understanding of the customer's need.**
- Scope changes are a necessary part of developing new products.

THINGS I LEARNED ABOUT WORKING WITH OTHERS:

- **A project team with diverse skills and experience yields the best results.**
- Emphasize benefits over features when seeking buy-in from stakeholders.

By contrast, Kim had the same takeaways from the experience as Jamie but also came away with some additional insights:

THINGS I LEARNED ABOUT DOING MY JOB:

- **Use small-scale, low-risk experiments to address unanswered questions.**
- Innovation isn't confined to product development.

THINGS I LEARNED ABOUT WORKING WITH OTHERS:

- **Senior-level support helps create momentum for "ground-breaking" efforts.**
- Clearly separate stakeholder needs from customer requirements.

THINGS I LEARNED ABOUT MYSELF:

- **I am effective at encouraging others' ideas and also building on them.**
- **I have a tendency to jump from idea to implementation.**
- My creativity shines when I face many limitations and constraints.

Learning agility is the key factor in what differentiates those who are able to extract the most learning from any given experience and subsequently apply it.

Learning agility is also a difference maker in career success. Individuals higher in learning agility significantly differ from others on a number of outcomes. Specifically, individuals high in learning agility do the following:

- outperform peers
- learn new information more quickly
- learn how to interact more effectively
- adapt well to working globally
- get promoted more frequently
- are less likely to derail

Over time, bosses and organizations recognize learning agile individuals as having the "right stuff" and as high-potential talent. As a result, they are afforded some of the most sought-after opportunities for leadership and career advancement.

Conversely, individuals who are lower in learning agility lack the versatility and adaptability of their more learning agile peers. They are capable of career success, but typically within more narrow circumstances that favor a specific set of skills. It's when situations change and new skills and new approaches are required for success that lower learning agile individuals encounter difficulties. They tend to cling to what's worked for them previously and don't recognize or heed the signals calling for new skills and new ways of doing things. The more resistant these individuals are to adapting, the higher their probability of derailing is.

The true secret to success for learning agile individuals is that they've combined their ability to learn from and apply experience with acquiring a portfolio of high quantity, high quality, and diverse experiences. This combination of skill and situation takes on exponential value when looked at over time.

To illustrate this, let's return to our earlier example of Jamie (typical learner) and Kim (learning agile). That was just one experience. Now imagine what that begins to look like over the course of years as the learning agile person not only learns more from any given experience but also goes on to acquire a greater number of learning experiences that are both high in quality and diversity. Graphically, it might look something like this.

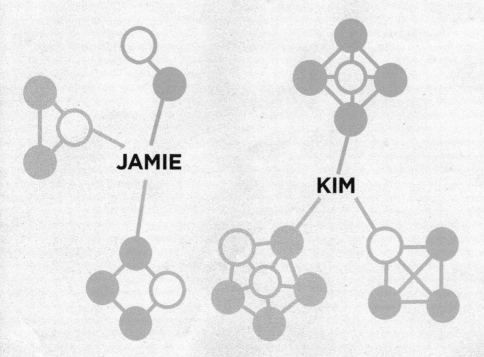

JAMIE

KIM

It's this complex, interconnected, ever-growing stockpile of lessons learned, primed for application, that allows learning agile people to enter new challenges and navigate their way to success. At the core of learning agility are four key sets of behaviors that are essential for learning how to learn from and apply experience. The rest of the book is devoted to explaining those behaviors and showing you how to develop them.

Learning Agility: Four Practices, Endless Possibilities

Learning agile individuals are distinguished by their willingness and ability to learn from experience. But they also excel at applying that learning to perform successfully in new and challenging situations. Put another way, learning agile people have "learned how to learn" from their experiences and made a strong commitment to seeking new challenges that allow them to both apply what they've learned and acquire new lessons for later application.

Few people who are learning agile have been explicitly taught the skills that have helped them become that way. Not surprisingly, they have developed these skills on their own and come to recognize these skills and their value as a result of experience. They are more likely to use terms such as "quick study" or "lifelong learner" to describe their abilities than say they are learning agile. Nor can they easily describe the specific behaviors that make up their approach to learning; it's simply "what they do when they don't know what to do."

CCL's research into learning from experience and the skills of those who excel at it has allowed us to decode the "unconscious competence" of most learning agile people and separate this competence into four specific sets of behaviors:

SEEKING

Developing learning agility requires an intentional willingness to immerse yourself in new and challenging situations that broaden and expand your experiences. Learning agile individuals see these situations as prime opportunities for new learning and growth. Furthermore, they are opportunities to seek out and embrace, not just to accept as each opportunity comes along.

SENSEMAKING

Learning from experience is a highly active and ongoing process marked by curiosity and a willingness to experiment. Asking "Why?" "How?" and "Why not?" are essential to gaining the insight and perspective that fuels learning. Failed experiments, and the setbacks and criticism that accompany them, are just a part of the ongoing journey for learning agile individuals.

INTERNALIZING

Learning doesn't end with the experience. Seeking feedback and taking time to reflect are critical for deepening insight and embedding critical lessons for recall and application. They also strengthen self-awareness, which is essential for dealing with future challenges in a realistic manner and staying open to new learning.

APPLYING

A lesson is not truly learned until it is applied. Learning agile individuals excel at adaptive learning—accessing principles and rules of thumb from previous experiences and applying them to navigate new and challenging situations. Swiftly adapting to new circumstances based on an understanding of what has (and hasn't) worked in other situations is at the heart of what distinguishes learning agile individuals.

These four core components of learning agility occur in sequence over the course of a learning experience.

SEEKING >>> SENSEMAKING >>> INTERNALIZING >>> APPLYING

They also layer onto one another so that as one encounters subsequent learning experiences, simultaneous pairings of Seeking-Internalizing and Sensemaking-Applying occur.

>>> SENSEMAKING >>> INTERNALIZING >>> APPLYING
                    SEEKING >>> SENSEMAKING >>> INTER

For the purposes of this book, we will treat them separately and sequentially, but it is important to remember that learning agility and experience are intertwined and many of the behaviors we describe flow together in a fluid and seamless manner, especially as you become more familiar with and skilled at them.

As you step back and consider the four components of learning agility, you've probably thought to yourself, "That seems pretty basic. So what's the big deal? Isn't that something everyone does on a day-to-day basis?"

That's essentially correct. The four components capture the basic pattern and progression of behaviors that inform experiential learning. The difference is that people who are learning agile engage in these behaviors at a significantly higher level of skill and commitment. And because they are constantly engaged in learning from and applying their experience, they are ratcheting up that level of skill and commitment on an ongoing basis.

It's the same with any skill that is shaped by and improved with experience. In this case, it's just the skill of learning from experience.

That's an advantage with developing learning agility. Experience is the essential ingredient and something we can all access. Since we understand how learning agile people seek learning experiences, make sense of them, internalize the lessons learned and then apply them, we'll show you how it's done.

Before we dive into each component of learning agility in more depth, go back to the experiences you recorded in the opening chapter and use the space below to record your memory and impressions of how you proceeded (or maybe didn't) through Seeking, Sensemaking, Internalizing, and Applying. Don't worry if you don't have a lot to record at this time; we'll dig deeper into each component as we go.

MY POSITIVE EXPERIENCE

Seeking:

....

....

....

Sensemaking:

....

....

....

Internalizing:

....

....

....

Applying:

....

....

....

MY NEGATIVE EXPERIENCE

Seeking:

....

....

....

Sensemaking:

....

....

....

Internalizing:

....

....

....

Applying:

....

....

....

Also, it's helpful to get an initial sense for where you might currently have some strengths or needs for development in the four areas. A good way to do this is to think of someone you know well who exhibits the highest levels of learning agility you've observed and compare yourself to them on key behaviors in the four areas.

Take a moment to identify this person, the type of versatile and adaptable performer they are, and what it is that distinguishes them in how they approach, learn from, and apply their experiences.

Next, for each statement that follows, use the following scale to rate this person you know who demonstrates the highest levels of learning agility ("Learning Agile"). Then rate your own learning agility skills ("Me"). [Note: Selected items can be found in CCL's *Benchmarks for Learning Agility* assessment.]

1 = Very Strongly Disagree   2 = Strongly Disagree   3 = Disagree   4 = Neutral
5 = Agree   6 = Strongly Agree   7 = Very Strongly Agree   DK = Don't Know/Not Applicable

Learning Agile	Me	
		1. Takes advantage of opportunities to learn new things
		2. Treats all situations as an opportunity to learn something
		3. Seeks experiences that will change his or her perspective
		4. Responds well to new situations that require him or her to stretch and grow
		5. Seeks out new and diverse work experiences
		6. Can make midcourse corrections
		7. Tries new approaches
		8. Is open to others' perspectives
		9. Acknowledges when he or she does not have expertise on an issue
		10. Tolerates ambiguity or uncertainty
		11. Responds effectively when given feedback
		12. Learns from mistakes
		13. Takes criticism well
		14. Reflects on and learns from experience
		15. Seeks candid feedback on his or her performance
		16. Is able to start over after setbacks
		17. Applies lessons learned from experience to new challenges
		18. Forms novel associations and ideas that create new and different ways of solving problems
		19. Adjusts to changes in circumstances easily
		20. Trusts intuition when solutions to problems are not clear

To identify items corresponding to the four components of learning agility, use the following key:

SEEKING: Items 1–5   INTERNALIZING: Items 11–15
SENSEMAKING: Items 6–10   APPLYING: Items 16–20

15

Looking at your ratings, what kind of patterns do you see? Do you rate yourself particularly high or low on one of the four components? What gaps between you and your learning agile colleague would you like to concentrate on closing? What pleases you? Consider these and other related questions as you go through the rest of this book.

The following chapters explore each of the four main components of learning agility. You'll learn the essential practices utilized by learning agile people that allow them to gain as much as possible from their experiences and enable their ability to tackle new challenges successfully.

Seeking

Learning agile individuals demonstrate the opposite of getting stuck in a rut. They are constantly exploring new pathways for themselves and others. Why? Because new experiences are like fresh air for their continual learning and growth. Without new experiences to challenge, stretch, and inform them, life loses some of its essence. It's as much a need as it is a desire.

Learning agile people are fortunate. Their track record of success in new situations means they are often sought out to take on fresh challenges, to which they invariably say, "Yes!" In the absence of new challenges being presented to them, they seek the challenges out. That's no ordinary thing. The seeking behaviors examined in this chapter require a willingness and commitment to take action, as well as considerable courage.

Exploring the anatomy of new, challenging learning experiences reveals why learning agile people are so eager to attain them. Research by CCL's Kerry Bunker and others provides a visual representation of what happens when we encounter a new learning experience.

ANATOMY OF A LEARNING EXPERIENCE

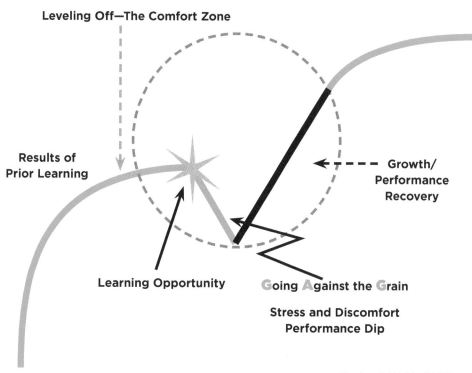

Leveling Off—The Comfort Zone

**Results of
Prior Learning**

**Growth/
Performance
Recovery**

Learning Opportunity

Going Against the Grain

**Stress and Discomfort
Performance Dip**

Bunker & Webb (1992)

17

Learning doesn't follow a continual upward trajectory. As we assimilate learning from previous experiences, we gradually enter a leveling-off phase. New learning opportunities jolt us out of our comfort zone. Performance falters and actually decreases while we struggle to learn and apply the skills required for success in this new situation. But the decrease is only temporary. As we gain skill and pick up some "wins" and the confidence that comes with them, performance and growth accelerate to a higher-than-before level until, gradually, a new status quo emerges.

However, this pattern occurs only if the new learning opportunity is embraced. Avoiding new learning opportunities yields a distinctly different, far less impactful pattern:

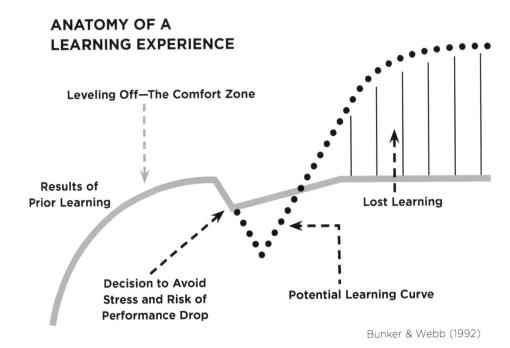

ANATOMY OF A LEARNING EXPERIENCE

Leveling Off—The Comfort Zone

Results of Prior Learning

Lost Learning

Decision to Avoid Stress and Risk of Performance Drop

Potential Learning Curve

Bunker & Webb (1992)

If we react to the new learning opportunity by choosing to stay close to our comfort zone and minimizing or avoiding exposure, we miss the uncomfortable plunge caused by going against the grain, but also the corresponding rebound in growth and performance. The end result is that we are pretty much the way we were before encountering the new learning opportunity. Most striking is what doesn't happen—all of the learning that otherwise could have occurred.

Learning agile individuals see the value in continually seeking and embracing learning opportunities that will propel them to ever higher levels of learning and growth. They have a knack for choosing opportunities that will yield maximum learning and further broaden their portfolio of experiences. And they do it often. This is the magic formula of high quantity, high quality, and diversity that was highlighted earlier.

Quantity should speak for itself. As for the other two variables, CCL's research has defined explicitly what learning agile individuals understand implicitly about the quality and diversity of their experiences. Let's dive a little deeper into each.

Quality

Quality emerges from several aspects of a learning opportunity. An exhaustive study highlighted what elements of a learning experience were associated with the greatest amount of learning:

- Unfamiliar Responsibilities
- New Directions
- Inherited Problems
- Problems with Employees
- High Stakes
- Scope and Scale
- External Pressure
- Influence without Authority
- Work across Cultures
- Work Group Diversity

The more of these elements that are present in any one experience, the greater the potential for learning. Let's revisit the positive and negative experiences you captured earlier. On the checklists that follow, tick off the elements that were present in each experience and reflect on what impact they might have had on the learning that occurred.

ELEMENTS PRESENT IN MY POSITIVE EXPERIENCE

- ☐ Unfamiliar Responsibilities
- ☐ New Directions
- ☐ Inherited Problems
- ☐ Problems with Employees
- ☐ High Stakes
- ☐ Scope and Scale
- ☐ External Pressure
- ☐ Influence without Authority
- ☐ Work across Cultures
- ☐ Work Group Diversity

ELEMENTS PRESENT IN MY NEGATIVE EXPERIENCE

- ☐ Unfamiliar Responsibilities
- ☐ New Directions
- ☐ Inherited Problems
- ☐ Problems with Employees
- ☐ High Stakes
- ☐ Scope and Scale
- ☐ External Pressure
- ☐ Influence without Authority
- ☐ Work across Cultures
- ☐ Work Group Diversity

Beginning with the landmark *Lessons of Experience* study, CCL has spent decades defining the types of learning experiences we encounter. The current list stands at 15. Each category is listed below, followed by a brief example.

FIFTEEN TYPES OF EXPERIENCES

Bosses and Superiors
Worked with a boss who was demanding and supportive

Turnaround/Fix-It
Fixed an underperforming unit or organization

Increase in Job Scope
Took on additional responsibilities without promotion

Horizontal Move
Transferred/rotated to different function/job at the same level

New Initiative
Created a new service/product/brand

Personal Experience
Played a leadership role outside the workplace

Crisis
Dealt with budget or financial crisis

 Stakeholder Engagement
Formed a partnership or joint venture across organizations

 Ethical Dilemma
Experienced ethical violation by a superior/coworker

 Mistake
Made a mistake that affected my team/unit/organization

 Cultural Crossing
Lived and worked in another country

 Career Setback
Experienced discrimination in the workplace

 Difficult People
Handled performance problems with subordinates

 Feedback and Coaching
Served as a mentor to someone

 Coursework and Training
Pursued advanced degree/certification

Return again to your two examples of past learning. Which experience category does each one fit best? Chances are that the negative experience falls into one of the final three categories (Crisis, Mistake, or Career Setback). These categories are referred to collectively as Hardship Experiences. We'll discuss them more when we examine the Internalizing stage. For now, it's important to understand that these are not typically experiences that you would willingly seek. They are quite valuable for learning but tend to find us, not the other way around. The first twelve are where you are more likely to focus when considering what direction you want to head next.

Now that you understand some fundamentals about why experience matters for learning and the quality and diversity of experiences that are out there, the rest of this chapter will introduce you to some of the key practices learning agile individuals use to make the most of seeking out new learning experiences. They are divided into three sections: Mindset, Skillset, and Toolset.

Mindset—Embrace every new experience as an opportunity for learning

The fundamental mindset driving Seeking behaviors is the belief that every new experience offers the potential for new learning and growth. Learning agile people hold themselves responsible for embracing new learning opportunities, refusing to take them for granted. Alternatively, deciding to stay in one's comfort zone and preserve the status quo of experience is a lost opportunity for learning.

Beyond this core belief, some other key elements of the Seeking mindset emerge:

The farther outside of one's comfort zone, the better.
Learning agile people are true believers in the aphorism "Life begins at the edge of your comfort zone" and often find the experience of living at the edge exhilarating.

Focus on the experience over the outcomes.
The real focus is on the experience itself and what learning it might yield. Learning agile people are less excited or concerned by where the experience will eventually lead or its career consequences.

Take ownership.
Once they commit to a new learning experience, learning agile people are all in. Not content to tentatively wade in or be passive bystanders, they put themselves at the center of what's going on and take responsibility for what eventually happens. This immersive approach carries over to Sensemaking.

Know when it's time to move on.
Learning agile people are a restless lot. They want to be where the action is and sense when they are starting to become comfortable in their current situation. That said, they are more about running toward the next experience than running from the current one.

Skillset—Explore. Risk. Challenge. Expand.

Try these behavioral approaches to improve your skill at Seeking. Some may require more practice than others, but all will help reframe the value of experience and orient you toward seeking quantity, quality, and diversity in new learning.

Find the limits of your comfort zone.

To get out of your comfort zone, you first have to know its boundaries. Explore both past and present circumstances to understand what experiences trigger an avoidance response in you and why. How might you reason with yourself to work past these "comfort zone traps" when future situations trigger them?

Take risks.

Some leaders are perfectly content to accept the status quo and remain safe within their comfort zone. In order to become a learning agile leader, you must be willing to accept new roles, pursue new opportunities, advocate for the unusual, and risk failing. Remember to focus more on the experience and less on the possible outcomes.

Define the opportunity cost of missed experiences.

Avoiding risk usually means that you're missing opportunity. Next time you encounter a new learning opportunity, consider what you might be missing out on if you decide not to take it. Also, what could that missed opportunity cost the organization?

Listen to your internal timer.

The leveling off phase of a learning experience is slow and gradual. Then next thing you know, you are "stuck" in your comfort zone. Stay alert to when the familiarity and the safety of the status quo kick in. Ask yourself, "Am I learning anything new? Am I getting stagnant?" Know when it's time to start seeking the next new learning opportunity.

Challenge yourself.

Identify your growth needs and then intentionally immerse yourself in situations that will push you to your limits in these areas. This may be uncomfortable and frightening at first, but it is important for you to reframe these threats as opportunities if you hope to gain the most learning from them. Seeking the first challenge is often the hardest—after seeking (and working through) repeated challenges, the confidence in knowing that you've been here before starts to grow.

Seek outside-of-work experiences.

Learning opportunities aren't exclusive to the workplace. Sometimes new challenges outside of work are even more valuable sources of learning, filled with surprising insights. For instance, one learning agile individual chose to put himself at the center of mediating a complex, emotionally charged family dispute over inherited property. The lessons he learned from this experience later proved very valuable in handling business negotiations back on the job that featured multiple parties with a lot at stake.

Expand your network.

New learning opportunities seldom just "happen," and those that you seek to create for yourself can be very difficult to make a reality. Remember: it's not all up to you. Other people play a key role. That's why it's important to establish a thriving network. Who you know can make the difference in what opportunities come your way and who you can reach out to for the opportunities you are seeking. Not all networks are alike. It is more advantageous to cultivate a network that is open, diverse, and deep. To learn more, check out the CCL white paper *A Leader's Network*.

Toolset—The Experience Audit

For learning agile people, success is more easily measured by the number of stamps on their passport than the plaques on their wall. They are caught up less in the constant striving for advancement and specific accomplishments and more in building an ever-expanding portfolio of experiences.

Learning agile people take advantage of the unique vantage point offered by their cumulative previous experience to construct a path forward. Looking at a learning agile person's resume, some of their choices don't always make immediate sense and sometimes appear like zigs and zags. But beneath the surface, there is a story that emerges, and it typically involves the search for the "next missing piece" in their experience that will add something meaningful to everything they've already done.

The experience inventory that follows is a useful way to take stock of your experiences to date and find that next missing piece that will provide the opportunity for challenge, learning, and growth.

Under the column labeled "Quantity" use the following scale to indicate the number of experiences you've acquired in each category.

1   I haven't had any experiences in this category.
2   I've had a limited number of experiences in this category.
3   I've had a fair amount of experiences in this category.
4   I've had too many experiences to count in this category.

Under the column labeled "Quality," use the following scale to indicate the depth of learning you've acquired in each category.

1   I haven't had any meaningful learning in this category.
2   I've learned a limited number of things from my experiences in this category.
3   I've learned a fair amount from my experiences in this category.
4   I could write a book based on what I've learned from my experiences in this category.

Quality	Quantity	
		Bosses and Superiors
		Turnaround/Fix-It
		Increase in Job Scope
		Horizontal Move
		New Initiative
		Personal Experience
		Stakeholder Engagement
		Ethical Dilemma
		Cultural Crossing
		Difficult People
		Feedback and Coaching
		Coursework and Training

Take a moment to reflect on the significant learning experiences that you've had and look for patterns and themes. For example, are there any areas where you see large discrepancies between the ratings for quantity and quality of experience? Next, consider what types of experiences are missing and what you might gain from seeking them out. What is the "next missing piece" that will enrich your existing portfolio of experiences?

Next, we'll examine the Sensemaking behaviors critical to extracting insights and lessons from the new experiences you seek out.

"Some of the best learning opportunities I've had in my career are when I initially went, 'You want me to do what?' or 'You want me to do this role?'... Seize the opportunity because you'll learn so much, and it's going to give you such a foundation to move on."

MARY BARRA
CEO, General Motors Company

MALALA
YOUSAFZAI
"WHY NOT ME?"

As the Taliban's repression threatened the ability of Pakistani girls to attend school, Malala had been fearless in joining her classmates to speak out for their right to an education. But the event that catapulted the issue to world attention—her diary for the BBC—might not have happened had she not sought the opportunity.

Originally, the BBC approached Malala's school seeking the insights of a teacher or an older student. All refused for fear of reprisal. It looked as if the diary, and a chance for their message to reach a broader audience outside Pakistan, might not happen. But Malala summoned the courage to volunteer herself, even though she had never before written a diary, because she felt this would be her only opportunity to get the broader awareness and support that just might change the course of events.

The tragedy that followed only encouraged Malala to keep moving forward toward new opportunities. Following her recovery from the attempt on her life, she took her advocacy global and established the Malala Fund, whose goal is to ensure that girls everywhere have the opportunity to receive a quality education. In a fitting gesture, she donated the award money from her Nobel Prize to finance the creation of a girls' school in Pakistan.

LEARNING AGILITY MYTHS
The All-around, Go-to Talent

Given the versatility and adaptability demonstrated by high learning agile people, it's easy to assume that they should be called upon for just about any challenging situation the organization faces. Not quite. Learning agile people thrive in many challenging situations, but especially new and unexplored challenges where both problems and solutions are ambiguous. Alternatively, some problems, while challenging, are more precisely defined and require a specific solution. These situations are better suited to an expert with a highly refined set of technical abilities. Think about it this way—if you run a nuclear power plant, you might want a learning agile person to explore promising next-generation applications of nuclear power, but you might not want them to address a design flaw in your safety procedures.

Sensemaking

So you've successfully sought out a challenging new learning experience. It's now up to you to make the most of the opportunity you've gained. As with most endeavors, what you get out is determined by what you put in. But what are you putting in, exactly?

Remember, the objective here is learning. Not traditional "book" learning, but real-life experiential learning. And the experiences that will teach you the most are high-stakes, complex, ambiguous, and dynamic in nature. You don't have the luxury of diligently absorbing the key facts or letting the problems and solutions gradually reveal themselves with time. It's time to dive in and start making things happen.

Learning agile people take a very active approach to making sense of the new challenges they face. They utilize multiple techniques, engage different senses, and even tap into their emotions to wrest insight and meaning from their experiences. The more they understand through doing, the more they learn and grow.

They don't take action for action's sake. The things they do, while often fast and fluid in nature, are quite purposeful. In many ways, their approach parallels what we often observe children do when they enter new situations. But for adults, those ways aren't necessarily conventional or commonly reinforced. Therefore, the right adult mindset is needed to unlock the wonderment and experimentation of childhood learning.

Mindset—The Constant Traveler

When asked about what characterized his attitude and approach to encountering new situations, one learning agile person put it this way:

> "You know that feeling you get when you first travel to a new country? How everything is fresh and exciting and confusing, all at the same time? Well, I try to capture that feeling each and every day and approach both new and familiar situations as if I am travelling in a new country. It puts me in this hyperstimulated state where new insights and possibilities reveal themselves."

The traveler's mindset permeates the thinking of learning agile people as they explore and navigate the new challenges they encounter and reinterpret the everyday. Their focus is concentrated on the journey, and this helps them frame what others might see as overwhelming as something exciting. The immersive travel theme carries over to other aspects of the Sensemaking mindset:

Leave it all behind.
Learning agile people favor approaching new situations with a beginner's mindset. They recognize that one of the best ways to learn from experience is to first try to forget everything you already know. They demonstrate the courage to be curious, even naïve, and absorb as much as they can from others' perspectives.

Get adventuresome.
You don't learn by virtue of just being there. Learning is an active, ongoing process involving some measure of effort, intention, and willingness. Venturing out of the realm of the comfortable and familiar and taking in as much of the experience as possible yields the most vivid learning.

Lost in translation.
Any extended trip to a far-off land will involve its share of cultural faux-pas, exchange rate miscalculations, lost-in-the-subway moments, and even the possibility of a misplaced passport. Learning agile people accept that errors, mistakes, and unpleasant experiences are part of any new situation. They embrace these as essential to learning and wear the scrapes and bruises of the experience with pride.

Anticipate learning.

Given the opportunity to contemplate a known learning opportunity
(an international assignment, a rotation in a different function, an
appointment to a cross-functional team), begin your mental preparation
by formulating questions that ready you for the learning ahead: How
might this represent a new challenge for me? What might I learn as a
result? How might lessons from past experiences apply?

Exploit ambiguity.

Ambiguity can be daunting, even paralyzing, for many people. Learning
agile individuals often engage in a clever reframing of ambiguous
circumstances. Instead of being inhibited by the lack of a clear problem or
solution, they find freedom in defining the problem and the solution in a
way that suits their needs. No rules? No problem!

Switch frames and lenses.

How you choose to look at a situation determines a lot about the insights
you form and the actions you take. Learning agile people carry with them
enough frames and lenses to open an optometrist's shop. They frame
(and reframe) the nature of the problem, the outcomes they're seeking,
and the approaches that may or may not work. They switch back and
forth between multiple lenses, including stakeholders' views, disciplinary
frameworks, and cultural values. All these lenses combine to provide a
multilayered understanding of the situation.

Start and adapt.

When you're met with situations that are initially confusing, sometimes
it helps to jump in and just start trying some things out. Try small-scale
experiments that will help you develop clarity and confidence over time.
Adopt the principles and practices of rapid prototyping so that you can
"fail fast" on your way to success. It's all about theory testing in real time.
One learning agile person observed, "You need to persist until your theory
of the situation and the outcomes of your actions match up."

Question internally and externally.
Learning agile people carry on a constant internal question-and-answer dialogue to support real-time learning. ("What's important here?" "How am I feeling?" "What's my intuition telling me?" "What are my actions telling me about what's working and what's not working?") They also ask others a lot of questions to inform their own curiosity. These aren't typically closed-ended, fact-searching, put-you-on-the-spot questions. They are meant to elicit insight and are often free of judgment.

Take a fresh approach to everyday experiences. Learning agile people find ways to discover the new in the everyday. This includes the following techniques:

• **Break up stale routines.** Doing things the same way over and over again, even if it works, is a detriment to learning and growth. Intentionally experiment with new ways of doing things. Observe what happens and monitor your results, including what doesn't work. Once new habits start to form, reinvent.

• **Reinvent.** When applying everyday solutions to everyday problems, stop to ask yourself how things might be done differently, especially if you didn't have the typical means to do things. Next time, give an alternate approach a try and see what the outcome is.

• **Question tradition.** Inefficient and suboptimal approaches often persist for a long time because they are accepted as "the way things are done around here." A better solution may be well within reach, but it takes someone willing to question the status quo and invite new ideas.

Prepare your mind and body for learning.

Learning agile people immerse themselves in new situations without losing control. They stay in tune and try to create optimal conditions for learning. Try these approaches:

• **Breathe!** Slow, deep, focused breathing through your nose, even for just five to ten minutes a day, supports your ability to maintain focus and remain calm in stressful circumstances.

• **Accentuate the positive.** A negative outlook inhibits the search for creative solutions. Look for the positive, even the humorous, in the situation and adopt a more optimistic lens.

• **Laugh.** An occasional burst of laughter brings oxygen to the brain, alleviates stress, and promotes resiliency. In group settings, it also cuts the tension that others might be experiencing and creates togetherness.

• **Show humility.** Learning agile people take what they do seriously, but they don't take themselves seriously. Humility and vulnerability are essential for working through the awkwardness and occasional pain that come with new learning.

"You are born a scientist. What does a scientist do? We look up and say, 'I wonder what that is. Let me go figure it out. Let me poke it. Let me break it. Let me turn it around.' ... That's what kids do ... We prevent that. We prevent these depths of curiosity from revealing themselves."

NEIL DEGRASSE TYSON
(astrophysicist)

Toolset—The Three *Ps* of Probing

Learning agile people are highly curious and often express this in new situations through readily asking questions. These are not just any questions, but inquiries that get them beneath the surface of the problem at hand and offer deeper insight into root causes.

The next time you find yourself in a challenging new situation, probe for insight by deliberately generating questions in these three areas:

PURPOSE: "Why ...?"

PRACTICES: "How ...?"

POSSIBILITIES: "What if ...?"

Don't limit yourself to just one round. Keep at it until you feel like you've gotten insight into the essence of the problem and started to uncover promising solutions.

Before delving into Internalizing behaviors, take a moment to revisit your positive and negative learning experiences. In the spaces offered below, record in as much detail as you can the specific actions you took and your reasoning behind them.

MY POSITIVE EXPERIENCE

What specific actions did you take to make sense of this situation?

....

....

....

Why did you approach the situation this way?

....

....

....

My NEGATIVE Experience

What specific actions did you take to make sense of this situation?

....

....

....

Why did you approach the situation this way?

....

....

....

Now that you're familiar with the mindset and skillset that characterize how learning agile people make sense of new challenges, look back at what you just jotted down and see if you can identify any of the mindset and skillset elements highlighted in this chapter. If you see little evidence of these or similar characteristics, how might their presence have affected the outcome of the situation?

....

....

....

....

LEARNING AGILITY MYTHS
Among the Very Best

Excelling at being learning agile promotes long-term career success but doesn't position you to be "the best" at a certain skill or capability. In fact, learning agile people tend to distinguish themselves as generalists rather than specialists. Once they've gotten a grasp of the skills they need to address the current challenge they're facing, their curiosity and restlessness lead them on to the next challenge and the next set of skills to be developed. As a result, learning agile people are better than most on a lot of things but seldom among the very best at any one thing. This is a key to their versatility and adaptability across so many different situations.

TOO MUCH OF A GOOD THING
Seeking and Sensemaking in Overdrive

You may have wondered if the behaviors associated with learning agility can be taken too far. The answer is that they can. This is especially the case with Seeking and Sensemaking. Taken to extremes, seeking out new challenges can give way to random thrill-seeking and experimenting, and risk-taking can devolve into reckless gambling. Don't be afraid to pursue big challenges or immerse yourself in them, but take the occasional pause to step back and measure whether you've gotten carried away or in over your head. If so, seek to make the proper adjustments and mitigate any damaging outcomes.

Internalizing

Learning is an ongoing process, not a discrete event. There is certainly learning that takes place in the moment and immediately in the wake of reaching key milestones. But even when an experience has reached a natural conclusion, the memories remain and the ripple effects of whatever happened may continue indefinitely. As a result, opportunities for learning are never really over.

Yielding insights from what has already happened can be challenging and requires some deliberate effort. Practices such as reflecting, seeking feedback, and embracing criticism take many of us out of our comfort zones and are therefore learning opportunities in and of themselves. Despite the discomfort they may provoke, they are essential to embedding critical lessons for eventual recall and application.

When we do engage in these purposeful acts of awareness-building, the lessons learned fall into three distinct categories:

The World of Work
(e.g., skills and perspectives to get work done)

The World of People
(e.g., interpersonal and social savvy to connect with people)

The World of Self
(e.g., managing one's thoughts, emotions, actions, and attitudes)

Some experiences will yield more lessons than others, and the proportion that fall into the different categories will also vary. But some experiences are more challenging to learn from than others. Not because the lessons aren't there to be harvested, but because of the negative emotions associated with them. These are collectively referred to as hardship experiences and fall into the specific categories of Mistake, Crisis, and Career Setback.

Hardships are different. With the other categories of learning experiences, the majority of learning comes from the success of meeting the challenge. With hardships, the learning comes from the *lack of success*. Many of the lessons learned from experience are external in nature ("What did I learn about handling my job and working with other people?"), while the lessons of hardship are often *internal* ("What did I learn about myself?"). The lessons learned from hardships often have less to do with the events themselves and more with *how individuals respond* to them.

"Follow effective action with quiet reflection. From the quiet reflection will come even more effective action."

PETER DRUCKER
(writer and management consultant)

Individuals who learn from hardship

- resist the temptation to put the blame on the situation or others' shortcomings;
- are able to step back from the situation to gain some clear-eyed perspective and recognize where their own mistakes and shortcomings contributed to the outcome; and
- demonstrate resilience in moving beyond the pain of the hardship experience and committing themselves to doing something about the personal limitations they realized.

Because hardships force individuals to come face-to-face with themselves, individuals often experience a significant shift in their self-awareness and better appreciate what they can and can't do successfully. They often get a significant dose of humility that increases their compassion and sensitivity in dealing with others' mistakes. Finally, surviving the hardship and willing themselves to move forward provides added strength to tackle new challenges and face future failures.

Unlike the other categories of learning experience, we seldom seek a hardship—hardship finds us. It is beyond our control. But we can control how we respond and how we frame it over time.

Whether you're seeking to mine insight from a hardship experience or a breakthrough success, the process starts with the right mindset.

Mindset—Ownership and Accountability

Going back to the mindset that drives Seeking—embrace every new experience as an opportunity for new learning—learning agile people have a deep appreciation for all that experience has to offer them. The "all-in" commitment and intensity that distinguishes the Seeking and Sensemaking phases carries over to Internalizing.

Learning agile people owe it to themselves (and the experience they've just been a part of) to see the learning all the way through. To simply move on and let the experience fade would be stopping short on their desire to gain the most learning and growth possible. Stopping to linger a while on what was learned and revisiting and reexamining the experience help cement the lessons that have already been recognized and surface new insights.

Here are some ways that the learner's sense of responsibility emerges:

Make a lot of mistakes, but don't make the same mistake twice.
Learning agile people are comfortable with stumbling their way to success. They distance themselves from the emotional sting, but they keep the memory of their mistakes—and what they learned as a consequence—close at hand. Successfully navigating similar circumstances in the future helps strengthen the takeaways from the original experience.

Know thyself.
Experiences, especially the most difficult ones, have as much impact on self-awareness as the specific knowledge and skills we acquire. Learning agile people value the insights they gain into their existing strengths and limitations and the resulting humility. It helps ground them and better prepares them for future challenges because they realistically know what they are and aren't yet capable of doing.

Never done.
Learning agile people see themselves as continual works in progress. They yearn to keep growing, keep getting better. Just as they themselves are never done, neither is their learning. There's always something further to be explored and realized and applied to the present, even if it is from far in their personal past.

LEARNING AGILITY MYTHS
Failure-Proof

Learning agile people achieve success across diverse circumstances and over the long arc of their careers. This track record for success frequently masks the fact that they experience more than their share of what might be considered failures. So they are in no way immune to failure. It's how they respond to failure—with deeper resilience, wisdom, and resolve—that distinguishes them and fuels their future success.

**Commit to a time for reflection and monitoring
your progress and learning.**

Our hectic, nonstop lives make reflection a difficult habit to form. Make
it a part of your routine or put it on your calendar so you can make sure
it happens. Record insights in a centralized place (e.g., in a journal or on
your smartphone) so you can revisit them later.

Revisit the experience.

Don't limit your reflection to just reviewing the outcomes—actually
replay experiences in your head in as vivid detail as possible to
incorporate not just what you did but how you felt as you did it. Also
consider others' actions and reactions. As you reimmerse yourself in the
experience, record your insights and categorize them.

Find an accountability partner.

Self-awareness and self-development require an ongoing commitment
to a process that will often feel difficult. Just as you can benefit from a
workout partner to increase your physical fitness, you may also benefit
from a partner who is willing to support, guide, and walk with you on
the path toward leadership excellence.

Seek meaningful feedback.

Go beyond "How did I do?" and "Give me some feedback." Surface
questions will get you surface responses. Ask people you trust to be open
to share specifics about what they observed, how it impacted them, and
what you might do differently in the future.

Embrace criticism.

It is, after all, a gift and a genuine window into how others perceive
and respond to you. Don't frame it as right or wrong or good or bad,
but as an opportunity for genuine insight and a means to calibrate
your behavior going forward. Let others know you got the message and
appreciate their openness, which will encourage future feedback.

Put setbacks in perspective.

Don't run away from mistakes and failures, but don't dwell on them either. Strive to get beyond the pain and disappointment and refocus on what can be learned from the experience and applied to future circumstances. Occasionally look back and evaluate the progress you've made.

Seek experiences that will enhance self-awareness and capacity to learn.

Different experiences yield different insights and lessons. CCL research has identified specific experiences that promote the development of self-awareness and "learning to learn." See if you can engage in some of these awareness-enhancing experiences:

- Trade responsibilities with a colleague and then serve as each other's peer coach.
- Work with colleagues to redesign a work process.
- Actively participate in the start-up of a new team.
- Take over a project that is in trouble.
- Work on improving a relationship with a difficult colleague.
- Work in a short-term assignment in another office/region/ country.
- Teach a course inside or outside the organization.
- Lead a benchmarking team that visits and learns from other organizations.
- Participate in a job rotation program.
- Start a new group, club, or team.
- Take up a new hobby.

Toolset—Be Grateful

Reflecting doesn't equal ruminating. It's about seeing the whole situation—both the negative and the positive—in fair measure. Of course, it's in our nature to dwell on what didn't go right. That indeed serves a purpose, but without a full appreciation of the situation and our role in it, opportunities for learning go untapped.

Focusing on the positive requires deliberate focus. Gratitude journaling is an everyday practice that can help us more readily see the positive in situations and ourselves.

Before you begin, take a moment to recognize the things in your life that you are always grateful for—loved ones, food and shelter, etc. Set those aside as "givens" on your list.

Going forward, take a moment to pause toward the end of the day for reflection. As part of that, identify three things (work-related or otherwise) not on your givens list that you are particularly grateful for and why they make you feel that way.

Consider how that realization makes you see the day and its events in a different light. What else does that reveal?

Before wrapping up with the Internalizing phase, revisit your positive and negative learning experiences. Use the vivid recollection technique highlighted in the Skillset section and see if you can "replay" the situation in as much detail as possible. Next, in the spaces that follow, record in as much detail as you can the specific lessons you took away from each experience. Try expressing these as principles or rules-of-thumb that you can apply going forward.

MY POSITIVE EXPERIENCE

Things I Learned About Doing My Job:

....

....

....

Things I Learned About Working With Others:

....

....

....

Things I Learned About Myself:

....

....

....

MY NEGATIVE EXPERIENCE

Things I Learned About Doing My Job:

....

....

....

Things I Learned About Working With Others:

....

....

....

Things I Learned About Myself:

....

....

....

IN THEIR OWN WORDS
Revisiting the Past to Reinvigorate the Present

Miguel recently moved a long distance for a new job opportunity. As he settled into his new life and formed relationships, he had the nagging sense that others were getting a limited view of his personality, skills, and character. In the midst of this, he made a two-week trip back to his former location. Reconnecting with friends and colleagues reminded him anew of who he really was.

Miguel reflected: "Being back in that environment really helped strengthen my identity. Things I'd sort of forgotten about myself— my agility, my creativity, my resilience—all came back to the surface. When I returned to my new job and my new life, I was better able to bring my 'whole self' to situations and show people who I really am."

Applying

The Internalizing phase focuses on the thinking and behaviors that promote capturing the lessons of experience. But learning doesn't end there. A lesson isn't truly learned until it has been applied.

Application is essential to being learning agile. If all the knowledge and insights gained from experience went untapped, we wouldn't really be any different than before and the challenges we face would persist. Application represents that all-important shift that occurs when learning is put into action. It's what allows you to eventually say, "I am now different because …"

The application of the lessons of experience is sometimes deliberate and planned but oftentimes spontaneous and unexpected. Because it involves the adaptation of past learning to a new challenge, it involves a mixture of flexibility, creativity, and intuition. It is challenging and sometimes frustrating but also yields exciting "aha's" and well-earned accomplishments. It involves overcoming boundaries, but part of the secret is to look past them.

Mindset—No Boundaries

Learning agile people avoid thinking in finite, categorical terms. They favor a more fluid and flexible mindset where boundaries blur and shift and where categories might be established only to be reshaped based on new input. Typical notions such as beginning and ending, success and failure, and should and shouldn't inhibit their ability to generate and apply solutions.

Here are some ways that boundaryless thinking emerges:

(Endless) possibilities.

In learning agile individuals' minds, a solution always exists. They just haven't discovered it yet. This keeps them in searching mode and considering "what if we?" and "how might we?" versus "we didn't" or "we can't" conclusions. They are also adept at building off others' ideas with the use of "Yes, and" responses.

It's all relative.

Nothing is ever as "new" as it seems. Everything is a matter of degrees of separation. Whether it's your own experience or someone else's, there's a connection to be made to something that has happened before.

Am I getting better?

Goals are important, but the drive to improve supersedes the desire to achieve. A steady focus on making progress and strengthening one's approach overshadows concerns about how far away the eventual goal is.

Actively search for parallels and connections.

In new situations, you don't have direct experiences to guide you. Instead, reference indirect or even seemingly unrelated experiences. What about them might be applicable to the current challenge you are facing? You never know what analogous solutions might emerge.

Focus on the familiar.

When facing a new challenge, it's easy to get overwhelmed by all that is different about it. Instead, focus on what you've done in the past that is somehow like the current experience. What helped you in those situations that might be applicable to the current one? One learning agile person referred to this practice as "improvising from a base of strength."

Trust intuition.

New and challenging experiences are characterized by ambiguity. When the problems themselves aren't clear, neither are the solutions. Relax the need to come up with "the" answer and trust your instincts to guide you toward "an" answer to start you down the path to better insight and better solutions.

Practice resourcefulness and perseverance.

In unfamiliar circumstances, first solutions rarely work. Sometimes second, third, or fourth solutions don't either. Be nimble in generating alternative approaches and gain insight from each attempt. Focus on the learning that occurs, not the frustration. Grit and tenacity will get you through.

55

Build your own brand of resourcefulness.

Everyone is different. Look at what's unique about you and how you approach hurdles. Over? Under? Around? Through? Over time, your signature style will start to emerge.

Explore unlikely combinations.

If you are particularly stuck on coming up with solutions, engage in "mash-up thinking" to stimulate new insights. Don't be afraid to be a little ridiculous or unrealistic. Do a "cocktail napkin" sketch of what this new solution might look like and see what thinking it inspires in others. Then see what new perspective you might have gained on the challenge you're facing.

Stimulate your senses.

Sometimes we think about problems and solutions in overly literal terms and get fixated. Find inspiration and reinvigorate your imagination by temporarily shifting your attention to metaphorical representations of the challenge you are facing. Images, films, stories, music, even smells—all can unlock something in your awareness to give you a new perspective and the ability to generate fresh solutions.

Measure learning and progress.

Addressing new and challenging problems typically involves a long journey. Frustration comes easily when you are only measuring yourself against the eventual outcome you are seeking. Instead, focus on the progress you've made from the beginning and what you've learned. Having and recognizing a few "early wins" is beneficial to navigating the long road ahead.

Toolset—Meaning Making Combos

It's now time for some tools to pull together different phases of learning agility. Remember, in real life, Seeking, Internalizing, Sensemaking, and Applying occur simultaneously.

G >>> SENSEMAKING >>> INTERNALIZING >>> APPLYING
SEEKING >>> SENSEMAKING >>> INTER

Each pairing involves a different type of meaning making and behaving. Sensemaking-Applying is all about being in the moment and taking fluid action as you wrestle with an immediate challenge. Internalizing-Seeking is more contemplative and tends to coincide with milestone events.

Utilize each of the tools below at what seems to be the appropriate moment in time so that you can gather the insights and formulate the actions that will keep your learning journey moving forward.

> "The past is where you learned the lesson. The future is where you apply the lesson. Don't get lost in the middle."
>
> **UNKNOWN**

MAKING THE MOST OF THE HERE & NOW
(Sensemaking-Applying)

How am I feeling about this challenge? How is that affecting my behavior?

....

....

....

How are others feeling/behaving?

....

....

....

Who can help give me perspective on the challenge?

....

....

....

How can I approach this with a beginner's mindset?

....

....

....

How might I frame it differently?

....

....

....

How can I probe for more insight?
("Why ... ?" "How ... ?" "What if ... ?")

....

....

....

How might I go about experimenting with solutions?

....

....

How am I making progress? What am I learning as I go?

....

....

What is my intuition telling me?

....

....

What does this situation remind me of?

....

....

What experiences in my past might inform my approach to this challenge?

....

....

....

MILESTONE MARKER
(Internalizing-Seeking)

When stands out to me about this experience?

....

....

....

Looking back at my performance, what did I do well/not
do well?

....

....

....

What feedback might I seek to get a better perspective
on this experience?

....

....

....

How far did this experience get me out of my comfort zone?

....

....

....

What have I learned about doing my job?

....

....

....

What have I learned about working with others?

....

....

....

What have I learned about myself?

....

....

....

**How might I apply what I've learned from this experience
to a new challenge?**

....

....

....

**What does this experience tell me about skills I still need
to develop?**

....

....

....

**What type of experiences might provide me with a meaningful
new challenge?**

....

....

....

What do I anticipate that I will learn from those experiences?

....

....

....

How might I go about pursuing these new experiences?

....

....

....

Let's conclude with one more look back at the positive and negative learning experiences you've been examining. Considering the lessons you've learned from these experiences, think back on how you've applied them to new challenges you've encountered since then. Next, think forward as to how these lessons might prove useful to addressing future challenges.

MY POSITIVE EXPERIENCE

How have you applied the lessons learned from this experience to subsequent challenges?

....

....

....

How might the lessons learned from this experience be applied to future challenges?

....

....

....

MY NEGATIVE EXPERIENCE

How have you applied the lessons learned from this experience to subsequent challenges?

....

....

....

How might the lessons learned from this experience be applied to future challenges?

....

....

....

Now that you've completed the cycle of examining these two experiences, in what ways do you think about them differently? What other experiences might be good candidates for reflection and learning?

....

....

....

....

....

LEARNING AGILITY MYTHS
Climb Every Mountain

Learning agile people apply their skills to successfully overcome numerous challenges, including situations where others have failed before them. That doesn't mean that they achieve eventual success with every challenge or accomplish every goal they set for themselves. There are limits to what they can do.

Limits are humbling to learning agile people, but not discouraging. They adopt a long-term view and recognize they've made a contribution to meeting the challenge that will someday be completed by others.

IN THEIR OWN WORDS
Getting Past Roadblocks ...
Literally

During an aid mission in Africa, Aaron and his team encountered a crisis. Access to an area in critical need of medicine had been cordoned off. As the roadblock remained in place, the need for treatment escalated while costs mounted and precious resources went unused. The team tried a number of ways to persuade the group controlling access, but to no avail.

Then they chose to redefine their constraints. A little digging revealed that only motorized vehicles were subject to the roadblock. How else might they get the supplies to where they needed to be? The team was able to secure some donkey carts, load them with supplies, and get them to the areas in need. It was a less than perfect solution—with a lot of extra time required and only about 10% of the total supplies able to be delivered in any one trip—but the team was able to prevail and make some progress until full access could be negotiated.

Embracing the Learner's Life

Learning agile people frequently describe themselves as continual works-in-progress. Another way to frame that is to identify them as lifelong learners. Under the right circumstances, learning agility is always on and never done. Learning agility is the product of all of one's experiences, can be applied to all aspects of life, and—if nurtured appropriately—can be sustained and applied indefinitely.

Embracing learning agility is both a tremendous gift and a heavy responsibility. It is not for the faint of heart. Lifelong learners experience many zigs and zags on their ongoing journey and plenty of stumbles and falls. But the diverse and exciting challenges they encounter and the wealth of learning they acquire make it worthwhile.

Learning agility is not a nice-to-have. It is becoming more and more of a necessity in today's unpredictable and ever-changing world. Learning agile people have the capability to handle new challenges with exceptional skill and are critical to addressing some of the most daunting issues in business and society.

Learning agility is more than pure skill. Willingness is essential to learning from experience.

Ultimately, learning is a choice. Choose learning ... and see what happens!

65

BACKGROUND

The origins of learning agility can be traced back to one of the landmark books of leadership development, *The Lessons of Experience: How Successful Executives Develop on the Job*. This ground-breaking effort uncovered some essential truths about how leaders developed at a time when there was very little established knowledge on the topic. Key insights from the study included the following:

- Experience is the best teacher, particularly challenging experiences that take place on the job.
- Some experiences are more powerful sources of learning than others.
- The more high-quality, diverse learning experiences one has, the better.
- And, most pertinent to learning agility, some people excel at learning from their experiences more than others.

The fundamental insights generated from the original *Lessons of Experience* research have been replicated and built upon across the globe for several decades. Specific to learning agility, that knowledge has been translated into different forms of assessment (*Benchmarks for Learning Agility*), learning tools (*Experience Explorer*), a forthcoming video-based eCourse, and executive education offerings (learning agility is one of the Fundamental Four competencies in CCL's Leadership Development Roadmap).

More recently, a new field of related research and practice has emerged called Experience-Driven Leader Development. The focus is on equipping organizations to most effectively utilize challenging on-the-job experiences as a strategic tool for leader development. To the extent that organizations can create and align the necessary systems and practices to optimize the ability to learn from experience, they can benefit individual and collective efforts to develop learning agility.

SUGGESTED RESOURCES

Bunker, K. A. & Webb, A. D. (1992). *Learning how to learn from experience: Impact of stress and coping.* Greensboro, NC: Center for Creative Leadership.

Center for Creative Leadership. *Benchmarks® for Learning Agility™.* (2015). Greensboro, NC: Center for Creative Leadership.

Center for Creative Leadership. *Experience Explorer™.* (2014). Greensboro, NC: Center for Creative Leadership.

McCall, M. W., Jr., Lombardo, M. M., & Morrison, A. M. (1988). *The lessons of experience: How successful executives develop on the job.* New York, NY: The Free Press.

McCauley, C. D. (2006). *Developmental assignments: Creating learning experiences without changing jobs.* Greensboro, NC: Center for Creative Leadership.

McCauley, C. D., DeRue, D. S., Yost, P. R., & Taylor, S. (Eds.). *Experience-driven leader development.* (2014). San Francisco: John Wiley & Sons.

McCauley, C. D., & McCall, M. W., Jr. (Eds.). *Using experience to develop leadership talent: How organizations leverage on-the-job development.* (2014). San Francisco: John Wiley & Sons.

Ohlott, P. O. (2004). Job assignments. In C. D. McCauley & E. Van Velsor (Eds.), *The Center for Creative Leadership handbook of leadership development (2nd ed., pp. 151–182).* San Francisco: Jossey-Bass.

Ruderman, M. N., & Ohlott, P. J. (2000). *Learning from life: Turning life's lessons into leadership experiences.* Greensboro, NC: Center for Creative Leadership.

Willburn, P., & Cullen, K. (2014). *A Leader's Network: How to Help Your Talent Invest in the Right Relationships at the Right Time.* Greensboro, NC: Center for Creative Leadership.

Wilson, M. S. (2010). *Developing tomorrow's leaders today: Insights from corporate India.* Singapore: John Wiley & Sons (Asia) Pte. Ltd.

ABOUT THE CENTER FOR CREATIVE LEADERSHIP

The Center for Creative Leadership (CCL) is a top-ranked, global provider of leadership development. By leveraging the power of leadership to drive results that matter most to clients, CCL transforms individual leaders, teams, organizations, and society. Our array of cutting-edge solutions is steeped in extensive research and experience gained from working with hundreds of thousands of leaders at all levels. Ranked among the world's Top 5 providers of executive education by *Financial Times* and in the Top 10 by *Bloomberg BusinessWeek*, CCL has offices in Greensboro, NC; Colorado Springs, CO; San Diego, CA; Brussels, Belgium; Moscow, Russia; Addis Ababa, Ethiopia; Johannesburg, South Africa; Singapore; Gurgaon, India; and Shanghai, China.

Center for
Creative
Leadership